The Mysteries of Power

AATIF ZAHEER

BLUEROSE PUBLISHERS
India | U.K.

Copyright © Aatif Zaheer 2024

All rights reserved by author. No part of this publication may be reproduced, stored in a retrieval system or transmitted in any form or by any means, electronic, mechanical, photocopying, recording or otherwise, without the prior permission of the author. Although every precaution has been taken to verify the accuracy of the information contained herein, the publisher assumes no responsibility for any errors or omissions. No liability is assumed for damages that may result from the use of information contained within.

BlueRose Publishers takes no responsibility for any damages, losses, or liabilities that may arise from the use or misuse of the information, products, or services provided in this publication.

For permissions requests or inquiries regarding this publication, please contact:

BLUEROSE PUBLISHERS
www.BlueRoseONE.com
info@bluerosepublishers.com
+91 8882 898 898
+4407342408967

ISBN: 978-93-6452-311-0

Cover Design: Sadhna Kumari
Typesetting: Pooja Sharma

First Edition: September 2024

Disclaimer

The information in this book is true and complete to the best of the author's knowledge. All recommendations are made without guarantee on the part of the author. The author disclaims any liability in connection with the use of this information.

Dedication

To those who inspire, empower, and illuminate the path of discovery:

This book is dedicated to the relentless seekers of truth, the courageous pioneers of change, and the resilient souls who dare to dream. To my mentors, whose wisdom guides me; to my loved ones, whose support sustains me; and to every reader, whose curiosity fuels this journey. May these pages ignite your spirit, ignite your passion, and ignite your pursuit of the mysteries of power.

With deepest gratitude,

Aatif Zaheer

Acknowledgement

Writing "The Mysteries of Power" has been an extraordinary journey, and I am deeply indebted to many individuals who have contributed to its creation and completion.

First and foremost, I would like to express my heartfelt gratitude to my family for their unwavering support and encouragement. Their belief in my vision has been a constant source of motivation and strength.

I am immensely thankful to my friends and mentors, whose insights, feedback, and guidance have been invaluable. Their expertise and wisdom have shaped this book in countless ways.

A special thanks to my school, Al Barkaat Public School (ABPS), for providing an environment that nurtures creativity and intellectual growth. The experiences and lessons learned here have been instrumental in shaping my ideas and perspectives.

Lastly, I would like to thank my readers. Your curiosity, passion for learning, and pursuit of self-improvement are the true inspiration behind this book. It is my hope that "The Mysteries of Power" will ignite the spark within you to dream big, think boldly, and achieve greatness.

With deepest regards,

Aatif Zaheer

Preface

The journey of writing "The Mysteries of Power" has been a remarkable adventure, one that has taught me the true essence of perseverance, creativity, and the power of belief. As a young author, my vision was to create a book that not only shares knowledge but also inspires others to dream big and pursue their goals with unwavering determination.

This book is divided into twelve chapters, meticulously designed to cover various aspects of power and self-development. From understanding the fundamentals of influence to exploring advanced strategies for personal growth, every chapter is a stepping stone towards achieving your dreams.

I am deeply grateful for the support and guidance I have received throughout this journey. Special thanks to my family, friends, and mentors who believed in my vision and encouraged me to bring this book to life.

May "The Mysteries of Power" inspire you, challenge you, and empower you to reach for the stars. Remember, the power to change your life lies within your own thoughts and actions. Embrace it, and let your journey to greatness begin.

With gratitude,

Aatif Zaheer

Introduction

In a world driven by ambition and the relentless pursuit of success, the understanding of power becomes essential. This book, "The Mysteries of Power," is a journey into the heart of what drives individuals to greatness and how they harness the power within themselves to achieve the unimaginable. Written by a young visionary, Aatif Zaheer, this book seeks to inspire, motivate, and challenge readers to think beyond the ordinary and strive for their highest potential.

As you turn these pages, prepare to embark on a voyage that delves into the mysteries of power, influence, and personal growth. Each chapter is crafted to offer insights, strategies, and real-life examples that will help you unlock your inner potential and navigate the complex world of power dynamics. Whether you are an aspiring entrepreneur, a student, or someone seeking personal development, this book is your guide to understanding and mastering the art of thinking big.

Welcome to "The Mysteries of Power" — a book that promises to transform your perspective and ignite the power within you.

With regards,

Aatif Zaheer

Contents

Chapter 1: Introduction: The Enigma of Power 1

Chapter 2: The Origins of Power 4

Chapter 3: Power Dynamics in History 8

Chapter 4: The Psychology of Influence 15

Chapter 5: The Role of Knowledge and Wisdom 22

Chapter 6: Power in Relationships 29

Chapter 7: Political Power: Governance and Authority ... 35

Chapter 8: Economic Power: Wealth and Control 40

Chapter 9: The Dark Side of Power: Corruption and Abuse 46

Chapter 10: Empowerment and Personal Growth 52

Chapter 11: The Future of Power 57

Chapter 12: Conclusion: Unravelling the Mysteries 62

Bibliography 66

Chapter 1

Introduction: The Enigma of Power

In the grand tapestry of human existence, few concepts have captivate, perplexed, and driven humanity as power has. From the primal struggles of survival to the intricacies of modern geopolitics, power weaves its threads through every facet of society, shaping destinies and defining legacies.

Power: it's the ultimate human obsession, right up there with Wi-Fi and coffee. From caveman arguing over the biggest club to world leaders debating trade deals (or who has the better tie), power has always been at the heart of human drama. It's like that invisible thread in society's sweater—pull it and everything unravels, revealing the true colours of human ambition, greed, and sometimes, surprisingly, altruism.

But let's be honest, what is power, really? Is it just the ability to tell someone else what to do, like the boss who insists on a meeting at 4:55 p.m. on a Friday? Or does it sneak into more abstract realms, whispering through the psychology of influence, the sociology of control, or even the philosophical ponderings of, "Why does everyone think my opinion is wrong when I'm clearly the smartest person in the room?"

In this exploration, we embark on a journey through the corridors of power, seeking to unravel its mysteries and understand its myriad manifestations. From the whispers of intrigue in ancient courts to the roar of revolutions that reshape nations, the pursuit of power has shaped the course of human history, leaving its indelible mark on cultures, civilizations, and individual lives.

History is littered with examples of people trying to grip on power. Take Julius Caesar, for instance—he didn't just settle for being a top general; he crossed the Rubicon and went for the whole Roman Empire, only to be taken down by his pest pals in a meeting that redefined "office politics." Or consider Marie Antoinette, whose famous (but misattributed) "let them eat cake" might have been the world's first recorded instance of missing the point entirely, showcasing how power can both elevate and isolate.

But power is a double-edged sword, capable of both empowering and corrupting those who wield it. It is a force that can inspire greatness and foster innovation, yet also breed oppression and sow discord. As we navigate the complexities of power, we confront the paradoxes inherent in its nature, wrestling with the moral dilemmas and ethical considerations that arise when power collides with principles.

But here's the kicker: power isn't just about ruling nations or "getting the last piece of pizza at a party" but it's about who get the chance to pick the first piece. It's a slippery, shape-shifting force that can empower or corrupt, depending on who's wielding it and why. It's the friend who help you move the couch but also the same person who "borrows" your Netflix password for a little too long. Power can inspire greatness and drive innovation, yet it's also behind every major meltdown from the school playground to the world stage.

In the pages that follow, we will delve into the dynamics of power, examining its sources, mechanisms, and consequences across diverse contexts and disciplines. From the corridors of political power to the boardrooms of corporate giants, from the intimate dynamics of interpersonal relationships to the vast landscapes of global affairs, we will seek to illuminate the hidden forces that shape our world and ourselves.

We will dive into many faces of power, looking at everything from political coups to corporate takeovers, and even those everyday power plays like deciding who gets control of the TV remote. Along the way, we'll dig into the ethical dilemmas, the tactics and the mind games—because what's power without a little manipulation?

Through anecdotes, case studies, and scholarly analysis, we will uncover the strategies, tactics, and ideologies that underpin the pursuit of power, shedding light on the intricate dance between ambition and ethics, authority and accountability, influence and responsibility. By confronting the complexities of power with curiosity and introspection, we strive not only to understand its manifestations but also to navigate its currents with wisdom and integrity.

Join me, as we embark on a quest to unravel the enigma of power, exploring its allure, its perils, and its transformative potential. For in understanding power, we may come to understand ourselves and our place in the grand tapestry of human history.

Chapter 2

The Origins of Power

To trace the origins of power is to embark on a journey through the annals of human history, where the primal instincts of survival intertwine with the complex tapestry of social dynamics and cultural evolution. At its core, power emerges from the fundamental need for security, status, and control—a need that has driven humanity since its earliest days.

Tracing the origins of power is like a binge-watching the longest, most dramatic series ever made, think of "Game of Thrones," but with more cavemen and fewer dragons. Our story begins in the chaotic prequel that is prehistoric times, where power was simple: whoever had the biggest muscles, sharpest spear, and could run the fastest from a sabre-toothed tiger was the king of the hill. Power back then wasn't about fantasy titles; it was about survival of the fittest or, more accurately, the survival of the fastest, strongest, or sneakiest. Imagine a hunter-gatherer society where the top predator wasn't a lion but that one guy who could bring home a mammoth for dinner without becoming dessert himself.

In the dawn of human existence, power took on primal forms, rooted in physical strength and prowess. In the harsh landscapes of prehistoric hunter-gatherer societies, survival depended on the ability to hunt, defend, and cooperate within tight-knit tribal communities. Here, power was often synonymous with the strength of arms, as individuals competed for resources, territory, and mates. The hunter who could bring down the mightiest prey, the warrior who could defend the tribe from predators and rivals—these were the figures who commanded respect and authority.

As humans put down roots literally and started farming instead of just running from things, power got a makeover. It was no longer about who could throw a rock the farthest. Suddenly the big deal was who could organize the harvest, keep everyone working, and prevent a single individual from hoarding all the grain. Enter the chiefs, elders, and shamans the original influencers. These were the people who could talk their way into power, claiming to speak to gods, ancestors, or whatever supernatural hotline was trendy at that time. Power became less about brawns and more about brains, charm, and the occasional well-timed miracle.

As humanity transitioned from nomadic lifestyles to settled agricultural communities, power began to take on new dimensions, intricately woven into the fabric of social organization and cultural identity. Chiefs, elders, and shamans emerged as arbiters of authority, wielding influence through a combination of charisma, wisdom, and perceived divine sanction. In these early societies, power was often vested in those who could navigate the complexities of kinship ties, religious rituals, and communal consensus, forging alliances and resolving conflicts through negotiation and mediation.

As humanity levelled up to ancient civilizations, things got extra. Rulers didn't just want to be in charge; they wanted to be Gods on Earth. Pharaohs build pyramids (basically the world's first extreme flex) to show everyone who was boss. These guys claimed divine rights because why settle for king when you can be a god-king? They wrote their own rules, raised taxes that would make today's accountants sweat, and built bureaucracies that were basically the ancient equivalent to customer service departments equally feared and equally frustrated.

With the rise of ancient civilizations, power became increasingly institutionalized, as rulers asserted their dominion through the establishment of centralized states, legal codes, and bureaucratic apparatuses. Pharaohs in Egypt, emperors in China, and kings in Mesopotamia claimed divine right to rule, legitimizing their authority through myths of divine ancestry and celestial mandate. These monarchs wielded power not only through military might and territorial conquest but also through the imposition of laws, taxes, and tribute, exerting control over vast empires and diverse populations.

But not all power was wrapped in gold and hieroglyphs. Behind the thrones, informal networks thrived, like the shadowy sidekicks of history. Merchants, scholars, and priests held their own power, manipulating the economy, spreading new ideas, and whispering in the ears of the rulers. Picture ancient Greece, where instead of TikTok dances, people were debating democracy. Citizens were suddenly empowered to vote, argue and sometimes throw vegetables at the politicians a tradition that's surprisingly relatable even today.

Power was no longer just about conquering land or commanding armies; it was about shaping minds, influencing decisions, and navigating the complex web of human relationships. The drive for control, status, and security has always been at the heart of human's story. From prehistoric muscle contests to boardroom battles, power evolves, adapts, and occasionally throws a tantrum when it doesn't get its way.

Yet, alongside formal structures of authority, informal networks of power also flourished, as merchants, scholars, and religious leaders vied for influence within their respective spheres. Economic wealth, knowledge, and religious piety became sources of power in their own right, shaping social hierarchies and power dynamics in ways both subtle and profound. In ancient Greece, for example, the emergence of democracy brought forth new conceptions of power, as citizens debated and deliberated in public forums, challenging traditionalist hierarchies and fostering a culture of civic engagement and political participation.

The origins of power are thus deeply intertwined with the evolution of human society, reflecting the complex interplay of biological imperatives, cultural norms, and historical contingencies. From the primal struggles of survival to the intricacies of modern governance, the quest for power has been a driving force shaping the course of human history, leaving its indelible mark on cultures, civilizations, and individual lives.

So, the next time you're stuck in a meeting that could have been an email, remember: that's all part of a grand tradition stretching back to the dawn of time. Whether it's a caveman trying to hog the fire or a CEO angling for a bigger office, the game of power is as old as humanity itself and just as messy.

Chapter 3

Power Dynamics in History

Throughout the annals of human history, the interplay of power dynamics has been a defining feature of societies, shaping the trajectory of civilizations and the lives of individuals. From the dawn of civilization to the complexities of the modern world, the quest for power has driven human ambition, innovation, and conflict, leaving an indelible mark on the collective consciousness of humanity.

Throughout history, power has been the world's longest-running drama packed with plot twists, outrageous characters, and more backstabbing than an episode of a reality TV show. From the rise of empires to the fall of kingdoms, power has shaped everything from the grandiose to the downright ridiculous. Whether it's a king claiming divine rights or pharaoh making everyone build a pyramid just to flex on his neighbours, the quest of power has driven humanity's wild ride.

In the ancient world, power often manifested in the form of centralized monarchies and empires, where rulers asserted their authority through divine right or military conquest. In Mesopotamia, the cradle of civilization, mighty kings such as Hammurabi of Babylon and Sargon of Akkad forged vast empires through military prowess and administrative innovation, laying the foundations for future systems of governance and law.

In ancient times, power was like the ultimate VIP pass: if you had it, you ruled the world literally. Take Mesopotamia, where guys like Hammurabi and Sargon of Akkad wasn't just a kingdom; they wanted empires. These were the original empire builders, laying down law, and conquering lands, and basically inventing bureaucracy. Imagine telling people you were chosen by the gods to rule, so taxes were not just a suggestion, they were a divine mandate. That's some next-level job security right there.

Meanwhile, in ancient Egypt, pharaohs were running the world's most elaborate cosplay as living gods. You'd think ruling an empire would be enough, but no, they also needed massive pyramids, intricate hieroglyphics, and entire priesthoods to remind everyone just how divine they were. It's like building a mansion just to impress your cat, but instead of cat, it's an entire civilization bowing to your every whim.

Yet, alongside the grandeur of ancient empires, power in the ancient world was also shaped by decentralized networks of trade, commerce, and cultural exchange. From the bustling markets of Mesopotamian city-states to the maritime trade routes of the Mediterranean, merchants, artisans, and nomadic tribes played pivotal roles in shaping the economic and social landscapes of their respective regions, facilitating the exchange of goods, ideas, and technologies across vast distances.

But power wasn't just about who wore the fanciest crown. While kings and pharaohs were busy carving their names into stone, merchants and traders were rewriting the rules of the game. From Mesopotamian bazaars to Mediterranean trade routes, power also flowed through the hands of anyone who could strike a deal, swap some spices, or convince a sailor to sail just a little bit farther. These were the ancient world's power brokers, peddling not just goods but ideas, technologies, and occasional cultural revolution.

As societies evolved and interacted, new power dynamics emerged, driven by factors such as technological innovation, demographic change, and ideological conflict. The rise of classical civilizations such as Greece and Rome saw the emergence of new forms of political organization, where democratic ideals coexisted with imperial ambitions, and the balance of power shifted between rival city-states and empires.

Fast forward to ancient Greece, where democracy was invented, and suddenly everyone wanted a say in how things were run well, everyone who has a free male citizen, anyway. Picture this: Athens, the birthplace of democracy, where debates were less about political correctness and more about who could shout the loudest. You had charismatic leaders like Pericles, who could win a crowd with words, and Alexander the Great, who thought, "Why debate when you can just conquer everyone?"

Yet, despite the grandeur of classical civilizations, the ancient world was also marked by periods of upheaval, decline, and transformation. The fall of the Roman Empire in the west ushered in a new era of political fragmentation and cultural upheaval, as the legacy of Rome gave way to the rise of medieval kingdoms, feudal societies, and religious institutions such as the Catholic Church.

Rome took it a step further with their "Go Big or Go Home" attitude. Starting with the Roman Republic's ideals of shared power and ending with emperors who were more concerned with being defied than democratic, the Romans didn't just build roads they built a legacy. They balanced a republic with autocracy, all while constructing aqueducts, arenas, and laws that still echo today. And let's not forget Julius Caesar's ultimate flex: crossing the Rubicon and declaring, "I came, I saw, I took over your entire government."

But just when you think you've got this power game figured out, the Roman Empire crumbles, and Europe descends into the chaotic, hot mess that was the Middle Ages. Suddenly, power is a patchwork quilt of lords, vassals, and kings who were often just one invasion away from losing it all. The feudal system was basically medieval Airbnb, but instead of renting homes, everyone was renting loyalty and land. Knights swore oaths, peasants paid taxes, and the Pope had more clout than a modern-day influencer with a million followers.

In medieval Europe, power dynamics were characterized by the feudal system, where political authority was decentralized among a patchwork of lords, vassals, and monarchs, each vying for control over land, resources, and allegiance. The emergence of feudalism as a political and economic system was shaped by a combination of factors, including the collapse of centralized authority in the wake of Roman decline, the rise of barbarian invasions and Viking raids, and the spread of Christianity as a unifying force in a fractured world.

Medieval Europe was a game of power. Jenga alliances built through marriages, treaties sealed with feasts, and betrayals at every turn. It was a world where being a king didn't necessarily mean you were the most powerful guy in the room; sometimes, it was just about who had the best connections, the biggest army, or the most elaborate set of royal robes. Power was constantly shifting, evolving, and sometimes even taking a nap between crusades and Viking raids.

Yet, even in the midst of feudal fragmentation, power in medieval Europe was also mediated by networks of kinship, loyalty, and obligation, as lords and vassals forged alliances through marriage, inheritance, and feudal contracts. The feudal pyramid, with its hierarchy of kings, nobles, knights, and serfs, served as the bedrock of medieval society, providing a framework for social order and political stability amidst the chaos of the Dark Ages.

As Europe emerged from the shadows of the medieval era, new power dynamics began to take shape, driven by the forces of Renaissance humanism, Reformation theology, and Enlightenment philosophy. The rediscovery of classical texts, the spread of printing press technology, and the rise of urban centres such as Florence, Venice, and Amsterdam all contributed to a flourishing of intellectual and artistic creativity, challenging traditional notions of power and authority in politics, religion, and culture.

The Renaissance, with its emphasis on individualism, humanism, and secularism, brought forth a new conception of power as embodied in the ideal of the "Renaissance man"—a polymath who excelled in multiple fields of endeavour, from art and literature to science and philosophy. Figures such as Leonardo da Vinci, Michelangelo, and Galileo Galilei epitomized this ideal, wielding influence not only through their artistic and scientific achievements but also through their patronage by powerful rulers and wealthy merchants.

Similarly, the Reformation, with its critique of papal authority and emphasis on individual conscience, challenged the hegemony of the Catholic Church and paved the way for the rise of new forms of religious and political authority. The Protestant Reformation, spearheaded by figures such as Martin Luther, John Calvin, and Henry VIII, shattered the unity of Christendom and sparked religious wars, political upheavals, and intellectual revolutions that reshaped the religious and political landscapes of Europe and beyond.

The Enlightenment, with its emphasis on reason, empiricism, and progress, further transformed the dynamics of power by challenging traditional hierarchies and advocating for principles such as liberty, equality, and fraternity. Enlightenment thinkers such as John Locke, Jean-Jacques Rousseau, and Immanuel Kant championed ideals of individual rights, social contract theory, and democratic governance, laying the intellectual foundations for the American and French Revolutions and inspiring movements for social and political reform around the world.

The American Revolution, with its declaration of independence and establishment of a democratic republic, marked a watershed moment in the history of power, as the fledgling United States of America sought to forge a new path based on principles of popular sovereignty, constitutionalism, and limited government. The drafting of the Declaration of Independence, the ratification of the Constitution, and the inauguration of George Washington as the first president of the United States all represented triumphs of the democratic ideal over the forces of tyranny, oppression, and arbitrary rule.

Similarly, the French Revolution, with its overthrow of the monarchy and establishment of the First French Republic, signalled a seismic shift in the balance of power, as the people of France rose up against centuries of feudal privilege and aristocratic tyranny. The storming of the Bastille, the Reign of Terror, and the rise of Napoleon Bonaparte as emperor of France all exemplified the transformative power of revolutionary fervour, as the forces of liberty, equality, and fraternity clashed with the vested interests of the ancient regime.

Yet, for all its revolutionary zeal and idealistic fervour, the French Revolution also unleashed darker forces of violence, extremism, and authoritarianism, as the Jacobins, the Girondins, and the Therm.

In the end, power has always been about more than just who sits on the throne. It's about influence, strategy, and occasionally, sheer dumb luck. Whether through war, trade, or occasional miracle, power continues to drive the human story, pushing us forward while occasionally throwing us off the rails. So, the next time you're stuck in a board meeting or negotiating who does the dishes, just remember: you're participating in the oldest game in the book, The Game of Power.

Chapter 4

The Psychology of Influence

The intricate realm of power dynamics is deeply intertwined with the complex web of human psychology, where perceptions, motivations, and behaviours intersect to shape the contours of influence and authority. From the subtle nuances of body language to the persuasive rhetoric of charismatic leaders, the psychology of influence encompasses a vast array of cognitive processes and social dynamics that govern our interactions with others and our responses to persuasion.

Power dynamics and human psychology?, it's like mixing rocket science with high school drama, where everyone's trying to sit at the cool kid's table. Imagine a world where social proof, reciprocity, and authority aren't just academic terms, they are the secret weapon of influence, hidden in plain sight, shaping every decision from your morning coffee order to your career moves. Let's dive into this psychological playbook, where power meets persuasion and everyone's vying for the upper hand.

At the heart of the psychology of influence lies the principle of social proof, which posits that individuals are more likely to conform to the behaviours and opinions of others in social situations. This phenomenon, elucidated by

Solomon Asch's classic conformity experiments, underscores the power of social norms and peer pressure in shaping our attitudes and behaviours, even in the absence of explicit coercion or persuasion. Whether it's conforming to fashion trends, adopting political beliefs, or following social etiquette, the desire to fit in and belong drives much of our behaviour in social settings.

First up, social proof. Think of it as the peer pressure that never quite left high school. Remember Solomon Asch's conformity experiments? It's like that awkward moment when you're in an elevator, and everyone's facing the wrong way. Do you stick to your guns, or do you awkwardly shuffle around because, well, it seems everyone else knows something that you don't? Social proof is why we buy things just because they're "trending" or join lines without knowing what they're for if everyone else is doing it, it must be good, right? Case in point: that time you spent $12 on a fancy latte because everyone else on Instagram was doing it.

Then there's reciprocity, the psychological equivalent of "I scratch your back, you scratch mine." Ever notice how you feel oddly compelled by something from the guy who handed you a free sample at the mall? That's reciprocity in action. Robert Cialdini nailed this concept this down: do something nice for someone, and they'll feel obligated to return the favour. It's the same principal behind those "free gifts" offers you can't resist. Remember that time you loaned a friend your notes and suddenly found them way too willing to help you move? Reciprocity works like a magic or blackmail, but friendlier.

Now, let's talk about authority. People are hardwired to follow experts, uniforms, and anyone who can convincingly point to a wall of degrees. Stanley Milgram's obedience experiments showed just how much people will defer to authority figures, even if those figures are telling them to do something totally bonkers. It's why doctors can wear the same white coat whether they're saving lives or giving dubious dieting tip sit's all about the "trust me, I'm an expert" vibe. And let's be real, if someone in a lab coat tells you to eat more kale, you're probably at least going to think about it, even if your taste buds are screaming, "No!".

Another one of my favourites is the principle of liking. Ever wonder why car salesman suddenly become your best friend? It's because we're more likely to say yes to people we like. They mirror your movements, compliment your choices, and suddenly, you're nodding along as they upsell you on leather seats you don't even want. This principle explains why you're more inclined to support that neighbour who's annoyingly charming at the HOA meetings or why you ended up at a Zumba class just because your friend with the perfect smile invited you.

Likewise, the principle of liking suggests that individuals are more likely to be influenced by those whom they find attractive, similar, or familiar. This principle, elucidated by Cialdini in his research on the factors that influence compliance, underscores the importance of building rapport, establishing common ground, and fostering positive interpersonal relationships as strategies for increasing influence and persuasion. From mirroring the body language of others to finding shared interests and values, the ability to create a sense of affinity and connection can significantly enhance one's persuasive abilities in social interactions.

Then there's the classic commitment of and consistency trick. Once you've said yes to a little, you're more likely to say yes to a lot like that "foot-in-the-door" tactic where a charity gets you to sign a petition, and before you know it, you're agreeing to host a fundraising dinner. It's why those "just try it for 30 days" free trials work so well one minute you're testing a streaming service, the next you're 15 seasons deep into a show you didn't even know you needed in your life.

Speaking of things we didn't know we needed scarcity! The ultimate FOMO fuller. If you've ever rushed to buy concert tickets, only to realize later that you didn't even like the band that much, blame scarcity. When something's labelled "limited edition" or "only a few left," our brain switches to panic mode. Marketers know this better than anyone; that's why they're always shouting about flash sales and last chances. It's not that really needed that fourth set of Bluetooth speakers, but when it's the "last one," suddenly it's a must-have.

Of course, cognitive biases also play their part in this psychological circus. Ever fall for a deal just because the "before" price was slashed in half? That's the anchoring effect, where the first number you see skews your sense of value. Or maybe you've found yourself thinking someone is competent just because they're attractive—that's the halo effect. Biases are like the sneaky understudies in the theatre of mind, subtly influencing every scene and making you believe that $50 burger is totally worth it just because Gordon Ramsay's face is on the menu.

The anchoring bias is another cognitive heuristic that significantly impacts our decision-making. It occurs when individuals rely too heavily on the first piece of information encountered (the "anchor") when making decisions. This initial anchor can disproportionately influence subsequent judgments and evaluations, even if it is irrelevant or arbitrary. Savvy negotiators and salespeople often use this tactic to set a high anchor price, making subsequent offers seem more reasonable by comparison.

Culture also butts on the psychology of influence. Ever notice how some cultures respect elders like they're all knowing sages while other questions authority like it's a sport? These norms shape how we respond to power and persuasion, whether we're bowing to a CEO or heckling a politician.

The psychology of influence is also influenced by cultural norms, societal values, and situational factors that shape our perceptions of authority, trustworthiness, and credibility. Cultural differences in individualism-collectivism, power distance, and uncertainty avoidance can significantly impact the effectiveness of influence tactics and persuasion strategies in different cultural contexts. From the emphasis on hierarchy and deference in collectivist cultures to the value placed on individual autonomy and scepticism in individualistic cultures, cultural factors play a crucial role in shaping our responses to influence and persuasion.

And let's not forget emotional appeals—the secret sauce of every good influencer. From heart-wrenching charity ads to nostalgia-laden political campaigns, emotions bypass your logic faster than you can say, "Did I just buy it because it made me feel something?" We've all fallen for the puppy-eyed plea or the feel-good story that had us reaching for our wallets before our brains caught up.

Moreover, the context in which influence occurs can significantly shape its effectiveness. The principle of contrast, for instance, highlights how the context of comparison can alter perceptions. When options are presented in a comparative context, the perceived differences between them become more pronounced. This principle is often used in marketing, where high-priced items are placed alongside more affordable ones to make the latter appear more attractive by contrast.

The concept of cognitive dissonance also plays a critical role in the psychology of influence. Cognitive dissonance refers to the discomfort experienced when holding conflicting cognitions (e.g., beliefs, attitudes, behaviours). To alleviate this discomfort, individuals are motivated to change their attitudes or behaviours to achieve consistency. This principle is often harnessed in persuasive communications to induce behaviour change by creating dissonance between an individual's current state and communication.

In the realm of persuasion, storytelling emerges as a particularly potent tool. Humans are inherently drawn to narratives, and stories have the power to capture attention, evoke emotions, and foster identification with characters and situations. By weaving compelling narratives, influencers can effectively convey their message, making it more relatable and memorable. The structure of a good story—complete with conflict, resolution, and a clear moral—can significantly enhance the impact of a persuasive communication.

Finally, the principle of personalization underscores the importance of tailoring messages to the individual characteristics, preferences, and needs of the target audience. Personalized communication, which takes into account the unique attributes and circumstances of the recipient, is more likely to be effective in influencing attitudes and behaviours. Advances in technology and data analytics have enabled more precise and targeted personalization strategies, enhancing the ability to connect with and influence individuals on a deeper level.

In conclusion, the psychology of influence encompasses a rich tapestry of cognitive processes, social dynamics, and cultural factors that shape our perceptions, attitudes, and behaviours in social interactions. By understanding the principles and mechanisms underlying influence, we can better navigate the complexities of power dynamics and interpersonal relationships, empowering ourselves to be more effective communicators, influencers, and leaders in our personal and professional lives. From leveraging social proof and reciprocity to understanding cognitive biases and emotional triggers, the study of influence provides valuable insights into the art and science of persuasion.

So, the next time you find yourself saying yes when you meant to say no, buying something you don't need, or nodding alone to someone's wild ideas, just remember you're not alone. You're part of the grand, hilarious, and sometimes bewildering game of influence, where everyone's playing, even if they don't know the rules.

Chapter 5

The Role of Knowledge and Wisdom

In the intricate tapestry of human history, knowledge and wisdom have always played pivotal roles in shaping societies, guiding decision-making, and influencing the course of events. While often used interchangeably, knowledge and wisdom are distinct yet complementary concepts, each contributing uniquely to the dynamics of power, leadership, and progress. Understanding their roles and interconnections is essential for grasping how they have influenced and continue to shape the world.

The saga of human history is like one long, epic soap opera full of power plays, brilliant breakthroughs, and the occasional catastrophic blunder. And at the center of it all? The dynamic duo of knowledge and wisdom. Think of them as the Batman and Robin of decision making: knowledge is all the gadgets, facts, and cool cars, while wisdom is the seasoned judgment that knows when to use the Batmobile and when to just call an Uber. They're distinct but inseparable, shaping leaders, driving innovation, and sometimes, saving the day. Let's take a wild ride through this world where knowing stuff and knowing what to do with that stuff are the keys to the game.

First, let's chat about knowledge. It's the building blocks of civilization the "LEGO bricks" of human achievement, from inventing the wheel to figuring out how to split atoms (and then hoping that wasn't a mistake). Knowledge is everywhere: it's why early scribes in Mesopotamia wrote down which crops to plant and why today's scientists are busy mapping the mysteries of the universe, probably while complaining about grant funding. Imagine it like this: you're at a trivia night, and knowledge is what gets you the answers "What's the capital of Peru?" Boom. Lima. You nailed it.

But then there's wisdom, the Yoda to knowledge's Luke Skywalker. Wisdom is knowing when to speak up and when to just let that drunk guy at the bar keep insisting Peru is in Europe. It's the nuanced, experience driven, hard-earned insight that helps you apply all those facts in a meaningful way. Wisdom doesn't care how much you know about quantum physics if you can't figure out how to have a decent conversation at dinner. It's the judicious use of knowledge, like knowing all the dance moves but not busting them out at your boss's wedding.

The interplay of these two has shaped some of history's most iconic figures. Take the ancient Greeks, for example. They were the original nerds, debating philosophy, science, and ethics long before it was cool. Socrates asked annoying questions, Plato pondered the meaning of reality, and Aristotle wrote about, well, everything like the kind of guy who just can't stop blogging. They didn't just hoard knowledge; they knew how to apply it, blending deep thought with practical wisdom. If knowledge were the raw data, wisdom was the killer app.

In the realm of governance, the effective use of knowledge and wisdom has often determined the success or failure of rulers and states. The ancient Chinese philosopher Confucius championed the idea that rulers should govern with wisdom and virtue, guided by principles of justice, benevolence, and propriety. His teachings influenced the Han Dynasty and shaped the moral and political framework of East Asia for centuries, underscoring the importance of wise leadership informed by deep knowledge and ethical considerations.

Fast forward to the Renaissance, and you've got Leonardo da Vinci, guy so talented that you almost hate him. He was like the Steve Jobs of his day, with sketches of helicopters centuries before people figured out how to make them fly. Leonardo didn't just know a lot; he knew how to cross-pollinate his knowledge, merging science, art, and a touch of mad genius. Picture him in today's terms: he'd be the type who's an engineer, artist, and start-up CEO, all while somehow still finding time to hit the gym.

In the scientific realm, the Enlightenment era heralded a new age of reason and empirical inquiry, transforming the landscape of knowledge and its applications. Thinkers like Isaac Newton, who formulated the laws of motion and universal gravitation, demonstrated how rigorous scientific knowledge could unlock profound insights into the workings of the universe. Yet, it was the wisdom to question established doctrines and seek evidence-based understanding that truly propelled the Enlightenment forward, fostering an environment where knowledge could thrive and be applied for the betterment of society.

Even in governance, the mix of knowledge and wisdom has been a make or break factor. Confucius taught that rulers should lead with virtue, not just intelligencea radical idea back when many leaders governed with all the empathy of a particularly grumpy dragon. The Han Dynasty took this to heart, setting up a civil service that valued not just book smarts but also the moral fibre to make wise decisions. Think of it as a leadership filter that would've prevented your office from promoting that one guy who always eats other people's lunch from the fridge.

Let's not forget the Enlightenment the age of "I think, therefore I am smarter than you." People like Isaac Newton didn't just sit around; they practically invented the modern world with their ideas. Newton figured out gravity (you're welcome, planet Earth) but also knew when to defy the status quo, challenging ideas that had held sway for centuries. It's like the ultimate combo move: first, learn all the rules, then break the ones that don't make sense.

Today, the digital age has put all the world's knowledge at our fingertips literally. We've gone from dusty libraries to Google searches that can tell us everything from how to make a soufflé to how to fix our weird Wi-Fi issues. But with great knowledge comes great... confusion. Now, wisdom is more critical than ever to sift through the noise, separate fact from fiction, and not fall for every clickbait article claiming to reveal "10 Things Doctors Don't Want You to Know About Bananas."

In leadership, wisdom is the secret sauce that separates the good from the great. Leaders with knowledge know the industry inside and out, but those with wisdom know when to pivot, when to pause, and when to double down. It's the difference between running a company and running it into the ground. Historical figures like Gandhi and Mandela didn't just have a sense of history and politics they had the wisdom to navigate conflict, inspire millions, and change the world without a single tweet.

In the context of organizational and business leadership, knowledge management and the cultivation of wisdom are crucial for fostering innovation, resilience, and competitive advantage. Companies that prioritize continuous learning, encourage diverse perspectives, and cultivate a culture of reflective practice are better equipped to adapt to changing environments and seize new opportunities. Leaders who demonstrate wisdom in managing teams, resolving conflicts, and making strategic decisions create environments where knowledge can be effectively harnessed and applied.

Even education systems are catching on. It's not just about cramming heads full of dates, equations, and facts anymore; it's about teaching kids to think, adapt, and, occasionally, question whether their textbooks might be just a tad outdated. Educators are emphasizing critical thinking and emotional intelligence, recognizing that the wise use of knowledge is what truly prepares students for the real world where problems don't come with answer keys, and life's pop quizzes are never multiple-choice.

In healthcare, it's not just about knowing the latest research but having the bedside manner and ethical judgment to guide patients through tough choices. It's why doctors aren't replaced by robots (yet), because no algorithm can replicate the wisdom of a seasoned physician who's seen it all and knows that sometimes the best medicine isn't a pill but a well timed word of encouragement.

The humanities and social sciences, in particular, offer valuable insights into the human condition, societal structures, and cultural dynamics. By exploring literature, history, philosophy, and the arts, individuals can gain a deeper understanding of different perspectives, ethical dilemmas, and the intricacies of human behaviour. This holistic approach to knowledge fosters the development of wisdom, enabling individuals to navigate the complexities of life with empathy, insight, and moral integrity.

In the realm of personal development, the pursuit of knowledge and the cultivation of wisdom are integral to leading a fulfilling and purposeful life. Lifelong learning, self-reflection, and the willingness to embrace new experiences contribute to personal growth and the continuous evolution of one's understanding. Wisdom, in this context, involves the ability to make choices that align with one's values, goals, and the greater good, balancing self-interest with a sense of responsibility and compassion for others.

The integration of knowledge and wisdom is also evident in the fields of medicine and healthcare. Medical professionals rely on extensive scientific knowledge to diagnose and treat illnesses, but it is their wisdom that guides them in making ethical decisions, communicating effectively with patients, and providing compassionate care. The ongoing development of medical knowledge, coupled with the wisdom gained through clinical experience and ethical deliberation, enhances the quality of healthcare and patient outcomes.

In environmental stewardship, the role of knowledge and wisdom is paramount. Scientific knowledge about ecosystems, climate change, and sustainable practices provides the foundation for addressing environmental challenges. However, it is the wisdom to recognize the interconnectedness of all life, consider the long-term impacts of human actions, and make choices that promote ecological balance that will ultimately ensure the health and sustainability of our planet.

In the arts, knowledge and wisdom dance a beautiful, sometimes messy tango. Writers, musicians, and artists don't just reflect what they see; they interpret it, weaving insights into creations that challenge, inspire, and occasionally bewilder. It's not just about knowing the technique sit about having something meaningful to say, like using a paintbrush to capture not just the world but the human experience.

In conclusion, the role of knowledge and wisdom in shaping human history, guiding leadership, and influencing individual and collective progress is profound and multifaceted. While knowledge provides the essential foundation of facts, information, and understanding, wisdom represents the judicious application of that knowledge, informed by experience, reflection, and ethical considerations. By integrating knowledge with wisdom, we can navigate the complexities of the modern world, make informed and compassionate decisions, and contribute to the betterment of society. From the pursuit of scientific discoveries to the cultivation of personal growth and ethical leadership, the dynamic interplay of knowledge and wisdom continues to shape our past, present, and future.

So, in this grand theatre of life, knowledge and wisdom are the stars of the show. Knowledge tells you that tomatoes are technically fruit; wisdom stops you from putting them in a fruit salad. The more we appreciate how these two forces interact, the better we can steer through the complexities of the modern world armed not just with facts, but with the savvy to use them wisely.

Chapter 6

Power in Relationships

The dynamics of power in relationships are intricate and multifaceted, playing a crucial role in shaping interactions, influencing behaviours, and determining the balance of control and authority between individuals. Whether in personal, professional, or social contexts, power dynamics profoundly impact the nature and quality of relationships. Understanding these dynamics involves exploring various dimensions of power, including its sources, manifestations, and effects on individuals and groups.

Ah, power dynamics in relationships—the ultimate game of "Who's really in charge here?" It's like being on a seesaw where one side might suddenly drop you if you're not paying attention. Whether it's in your personal life, at work, or even with that one friend who always insists on picking the restaurant (and it's always sushi), power dynamics shape how we interact, influence, and occasionally, annoy each other. To understand how this game is played, we need to dig into the different types of power moves, what gives someone the upper hand, and why sometimes you just have to let them feel like the boss (even when you know they're not.

Power is basically the ability to do something they wouldn't normally do like convincing your spouse that folding laundry is a "bonding experience." This can come from many places: your position, knowledge, resources, or just the sheer force of your irresistible seduction (we're looking at your charismatic types). It's the reason your boss's lame jokes get polite laughs, while your equally lame jokes gets a cold, hard stare. Power dynamics are everywhere, shaping relationships like an invisible hand that sometimes feel more like a poke in the ribs.

The Many Flavours of Power

Let's start with Positional power, the ultimate "Because I said so" of the workplace. It's what makes your manager feel justified in sending you emails labelled "URGENT" at 4:59 p.m. on a Friday. This kind of power comes from being the one with the title, the corner office, or at least the best parking spot. People with positional power can make decisions that affect others, like deciding who gets the plum assignments and who gets stuck with cleaning out the office fridge. It's institutional, recognized, or sometimes deeply resented.

Then there's Expert power—think of it as your nerdy friend's superpower. It's all about knowing your stuff. If you've ever deferred to an IT guy who speaks fluent "tech jargon" just to fix your Wi-Fi, you've experienced expert power in action. This power doesn't come from rank; it comes from knowledge and skills, and it often commands respect (or at least grudging admiration) because it's genuinely earned. If you're the office's go-to person for Excel wizardry, congratulations, you've got expert power. Just don't let it go your head; no one likes a spreadsheet tyrant.

Resource power is like holding the keys to the kingdom or at least the keys to the company's snack closet. It's all about control over valuable resources like money, information, or that family secret recipe for killer brownies. People who control resources can wield influence simply by deciding who gets what and when. It's why your uncle who always "forgets his wallet" somehow has the power to decide which bar you'll end up at. In relationships, this can lead to serious power imbalances, like when one person controls all the finances while other has to ask for permission to buy a latte.

Charismatic power, or "you're so charming, I'd probably follow you anywhere," is a whole different beast. It's that inexplicable draw some people have that makes others want to be around them, listen to them, or occasionally buy what they're selling (metaphorically or literally). Think of charismatic power as the secret sauce behind every great leader, celebrity, and your one friend who can talk their way into and out of just about anything. It's not something you can just study; it's about personality, communication, and often a good dose of luck.

Finally, there's Social power, the "It's not what you know, it's who you know" dynamic. This one is all about connections, networking, and the subtle art of working the room like a pro. It's why your co-worker's second cousin's roommate's uncle just so happens to be the best person for that new job opening. People with strong social networks can pull strings, rally support, and spread influence faster than you say, "Let's connect on LinkedIn."

The Seesaw of Power: Ups, Downs, and Drama

Power in relationships isn't set in stone; it shifts like the sand at the beach, and not always in predictable ways.

Sometimes power balances out like when you and your best friend take turns being the one to pick up the tab. Other times, it's a tug-of-war, with one person pulling a little harder while the other pretends they don't mind. In healthy relationships, power is balanced and shared, meaning both parties feel heard, respected, and valued. It's the difference between "Let's figure this out together" and "We're doing it my way because I'm louder."

But when power gets lopsided, watch out. In professional settings, this can mean anything from a micromanaging boss who treats you like an intern or a toxic office culture where everyone's just out for themselves. In personal relationships, it can manifest as manipulation, coercion, or that one friend who insists on doing things there way "because they know best." Spoiler alert: They usually don't.

Take, for example, a classic power play in relationships: the "remote control war." One partner wields power simply by always holding the remote, deciding what to watch, and never letting go. It's subtle, but there's a tiny, blinking metaphor for larger control issues at play. And don't even get started on the "who controls the thermostat" debate; wars have been fought over less.

Fixing the Power Balance: Communication, Compromise, and Maybe A Little Therapy

Healthy power dynamics hinge on good communication. This mean actually listening to other person, not just waiting for your turn to talk and being honest about your needs and boundaries. It's like being on a team where everyone's role matters and no one's just there to look pretty (though, hey, if that's your thing, no judgement).

Empowerment is another key ingredient. It's not about one person giving up all control but about both parties feeling capable, respected, and free to express themselves. It's like teaching your teenager to drive: nerve-wrecking, sure, but necessary if you want them to eventually get somewhere on their own. In relationships, empowerment looks like supporting each other's goals, cheering on personal growth, and occasionally, letting someone else steer the ship without grabbing the wheel.

Conflict resolution is also crucial because, let's face it, no relationship is conflict-free. But how you handle disagreements says a lot about the balance of power. It's not about winning the argument; it's about finding a way forward where no one feels bulldozed. And sometimes the best conflict resolution strategy is simple, "You know what? Let's agree that pineapple does not belong on pizza, and move on."

Cultural and societal norms also influence power dynamics in relationships. Different cultures have varying expectations and norms regarding gender roles, authority, and hierarchy, which can shape how power is perceived and exercised in relationships. For example, traditional gender roles may dictate that men hold more power in certain relationships, while women are expected to be submissive or compliant. Challenging and redefining these norms is essential for promoting gender equality and healthy power dynamics in relationships.

The role of empathy in power dynamics cannot be overstated. Empathy involves understanding and sharing the feelings of others, which can help bridge power gaps and foster connection and trust. Empathetic individuals are more likely to use their power responsibly and consider the impact of their actions on others. Empathy also enhances communication and conflict resolution, making it easier to navigate power dynamics in relationships.

In conclusion, power in relationships is a complex and multifaceted phenomenon that influences interactions, behaviours, and outcomes. Understanding the various sources and manifestations of power, as well as the importance of balanced power dynamics, effective communication, and empowerment, is essential for fostering healthy, equitable relationships. By recognizing and addressing power imbalances, promoting mutual respect and empathy, and cultivating skills in conflict resolution and communication, individuals can navigate power dynamics more effectively and create positive, supportive relationships in both personal and professional contexts.

In the end, power dynamics in relationships are like an endless chess game where every move counts, but sometimes, it's okay to call a truce and just play checkers instead. Recognizing and adjusting these dynamics can turn power struggles into power partnerships, where both sides work together, lift each other up, and maybe, just maybe, learn to share the remote.

Chapter 7

Political Power: Governance and Authority

Political power, where do we start? It's like the ultimate chess game, except the board is the whole country, and the prices are people, laws, money and sometimes, just plain audacity. Imagine a giant game of Monopoly where the banker makes the rules, the players buy influence instead of properties, and every now and then, someone flips the board when things don't go their way. At it's core, political power is all about who gets to call the shots, make the rules, and decide how the pie is sliced. Let's dive into the messy, fascinating the world of power plays, shady deals, and the occasional heroic stands.

At it's heart, political power is about influencing or controlling the behaviour of people and institutions within a political system. It's why some politicians can charm their way into a room while others bulldoze their way through it, leaving everyone scrambling to keep up. This power comes from all sorts of places—legal authority, brute force, money, and, of course, the magical power of a really convincing argument (or a very loud megaphone). Think of political power as the secret ingredient that keeps the whole system running, sometimes smoothly, often chaotically, and occasionally with the finesse of a runaway train.

One of the main sources of power is legal authority "because it's in the rules" kind of power. This is the respectable sort, wrapped up in laws, constitutions, and a lot of paperwork. It's the ultimate permission slip, saying, "Yes, you get to the boss." In democracies, legal authority comes from the people elections!, while in authoritarian regimes, it's more of a "sit down, shut up, and don't ask questions" vibe. Either way, it's the foundation that lets leaders lead, even if sometimes it feels like they're reading us straight into a dumpster fire.

Then we've Coercive power, which is basically the "do what I say, or else" approach. Remember Max Weber's idea about the state's monopoly on the legitimate use of violence? It's like saying the government has the only keys to the big guns, handcuffs, and those tear gas canisters they break out at protests. Coercive power is crucial for keeping order, think police, military, and your local traffic cop. But when it's abused, it's less "protective and serve" and more "intimidate and control." Overdo it, and you end up with a recipe for revolt faster than you can say "Viva la Revolución!"

Economic power, meanwhile, is the rich kid at the political party throwing cash around to get what they want. Control over money, land, or just the ability to bankroll a few campaign ads gives you a major say in how things are run. It's why billionaires, lobbyists, and special interest groups seem to have their fingers in every political pie. And let's not forget: when you can buy influence, you're not just playing the game you're rewriting the rulebook.

Next up is ideological power, or the "let's win hearts and minds strategy". It's the art of convincing people that your vision of the world is the right one, whether it's through a stirring speech, a catchy slogan, or a carefully crafted propaganda campaign. Ideologies shape how we see the world, influencing everything from voting habits to what we think is "common sense". Think of it as the brainwashing... but with more subtlety. Political leaders use ideological power to rally support, justify their actions, and keep the masses in line like a motivational speaker who's really good at hiding ulterior motives.

To see political power in action, you only have to look as far as your nearest government building or let's be honest, your social media feed. Take, for example, the classic filibuster in U.S. politics: a senator stands up and talks for hours about anything from their love of cats to their grandmother's lasagna recipe just to delay a vote. It's a legal power move so ridiculous it belongs in a sitcom, but it works. Political power isn't just about making laws; it's knowing about how to bend, twist, and occasionally tie them in knots to get what you want.

Or think about an authoritarian governance—the ultimate "my way or the highway" approach. Here, political power is concentrated in one person or a small group, and dissent is not just discouraged; it's downright dangerous. Imagine a political system where everyday feels like an episode of "Survivor," but instead of getting voted off the island, you get exiled, jailed, or worse. Authoritarian leaders hold onto power through force, propaganda, and occasionally just by being so fearsome that no one dares to speak out. It's efficient, sure, but it's also like playing with fire—sooner or later, someone gets burned.

In contrast, authoritarian governance concentrates political power in the hands of a single leader or a small group, often characterized by limited political pluralism, suppression of dissent, and centralized control over state institutions. Authoritarian regimes may use coercion, propaganda, and patronage to maintain control and suppress opposition. While authoritarian governance can provide stability and efficiency, it often comes at the cost of political freedoms, human rights, and accountability.

And then there's the international stage, where political power isn't just about what happens within borders but also about flexing muscles abroad. Think trade wars, military alliances, and no one's sure who's holding the best cards. Globalization has made political power a game of 4D chess, with moves happening on multiple levels, from the local Mayor's office to the United Nations Security Council.

All the heart of all this political drama is governance— the nuts and the bolts of how power is actually used to run things. Good governance is like good plumbing: you only notice it when it's not working, like when corruption clogs the pipes or transparency goes down the drain. In democratic systems, governance involves checks and balances, making sure that no one has too much power for too long. It's why we have parliaments, courts, and watchdogs organizations keeping an eye on the game.

Political power is also shaped by social movements and civil society, which can challenge and transform existing power structures. Social movements, such as the civil rights movement, feminist movement, and environmental movement, mobilize collective action to advocate for social change and hold political leaders accountable. Civil society organizations, including non-profits, advocacy groups, and grassroots organizations, play a crucial role in representing diverse interests, promoting transparency, and enhancing civic participation.

But governance isn't just about keeping power in check; it's about making sure that power serves the people. It's like being the referee in a never-ending soccer match—no one's truly happy with you, but without you, it's chaos. Effective governance means balancing all these different types of power - legal, coercive, economic, and ideological to create a system that's accountable, responsive, and maybe, just maybe, fair.

Technological advancements have also transformed the landscape of political power and governance. The rise of digital technologies, social media, and data analytics has reshaped how political actors communicate, mobilize support, and influence public opinion. While these technologies offer new opportunities for engagement and transparency, they also pose challenges related to misinformation, surveillance, and cyber threats. The impact of technology on political power and governance continues to evolve, requiring adaptive strategies and regulations.

Political power isn't just about who sits on the big chair; it's about the entire structure of influence that keeps societies ticking. From the grandeur of parliamentary debates to the backroom deals nobody wants to admit happen, power is the currency that buys action, change, and occasionally, a scandal or two. Understanding political power is like trying to figure out the rules to a game that's always changing and where some of the players are cheating. But hey, isn't that what makes politics so endlessly fascinating? So the next time you see a political power in action, grab your popcorn. You're watching history and maybe a little bit of chaos unfold.

Chapter 8

Economic Power: Wealth and Control

Economic power—where the real world plays Monopoly, but instead of hotels, people buy influence, control governments, and occasionally decide if we get the new iPhone or not. Imagine a game where whoever has the most cash doesn't just win but the set the rules, bribe the banker, and occasionally just straight-up print more money. From corporate giants to financial wizards, economic power is the real MVP shaping our world, often in ways that make us wonder who's really in charge.

At its core, Economic power is all about who controls the money and resources. Picture a puppet master pulling the strong behind the curtain: it's not just governments and big-name billionaires, but corporations, banks, and sometimes that one guy who got into Bitcoin early. It's the power to influence markets, fund policies, and, let's face it, make decisions that affect everyone's lives. Got wealth? You've got the backstage pass to the show.

Wealth accumulation is the classic "money makes the world go around" scenario. Those who have it can invest in businesses, control markets, and even fund political campaigns that suspiciously align with their interests.

Remember that scene in "The Wolf of Wall Street" where Leonardo DiCaprio throws cash around like confetti? Now picture that, but with real-life consequences: the rich getting richer, while the rest of us just hope our pay checks last until payday.

Corporations are like the superheroes (or supervillains, depending on your perspectives) of economic power. They employ millions, create products, and occasionally ruin your day with a "mandatory software update." Multinational Corporations (MNCs) can influence global trade policies, dictate employment conditions, and casually lobby governments like they're ordering coffee. Remember when Amazon went city-hopping to find a new HQ, making cities compete by offering tax breaks like free samples at Costco? That's corporate power flexing its muscles.

And then there are banks and financial institutions—imagine the world's biggest piggy banks, but with lasers and a suspicious interest in your credit score. Central banks, like the Federal Reserve, have the power to control interest rates, stabilize economies, and occasionally give everyone a collective panic by adjusting inflation targets. It's like playing Jenga with the global economy—one wrong move, and everyone's savings tremble.

Take a look at Apple, the trillion-dollar tech behemoth. Not only do they have more cash than some countries, but they also dictate terms with suppliers, influence global labour markets, and have every city vying for their next store like it's Super Bowl. They've turned "planned obsolescence" into a business model and made us all willingly but slightly different versions of the same product every year. Apple's economic power isn't just in dollars; it's in shaping consumer behaviour and making you feel that you need that new gadget even if your old device is working properly.

Governments, too, are big players in this power game. Through taxes, spending, and regulations, they decide who gets what slice of the economic pie. Want a subsidy for your struggling industry? Better have a good lobbyist, or better yet, be a crucial swing state during an election year. Fiscal policies shape economies in ways that go way beyond budgets; they define who wins and who loses in the grand economic tug-of-war.

Trade and Globalization? That's where it really gets interesting. Picture a global bazaar where countries trade not just goods, but influence and power. Free trade agreements are like secret club memberships: great if you're in, frustrating if you're out. Developed nations often get the best seats at the table, while developing countries are left hustling at the fringes, trying to sell their goods without breaking the rules set by the big boys. It's like being invited to a potluck but told you can only bring napkins.

In today's world, it's not just money that's power it's information. Companies like Google, Amazon and Facebook aren't just tech giants; they're data overlords. With the ability to track, analyse, and manipulate consumer behaviour, they're redefining what it means to have economic power. Your search history isn't just embarrassing; it's a goldmine of insights that these companies use to shape markets, target ads, and even influence elections. Remember when you talked about hiking boots, and suddenly every ad is for outdoor gear? Yeah, that's economic power at work, and it knows what you're thinking before you do.

The concentration of economic power raises important questions about inequality and social justice. Economic disparities, driven by differences in wealth, income, and access to resources, can lead to unequal opportunities and outcomes. Wealth concentration in the hands of a few can exacerbate social divisions, limit social mobility, and undermine democratic processes. Addressing these disparities requires policies and interventions aimed at promoting economic inclusion, equitable distribution of resources, and access to opportunities for all segments of society.

Economic power also influences political processes and governance. Wealthy individuals and corporations can exert significant influence over political campaigns, policy decisions, and legislative agendas through lobbying, political donations, and advocacy. This intersection of economic and political power can lead to policy outcomes that favour the interests of the wealthy and powerful, potentially at the expense of broader public interests. Transparency, accountability, and regulatory measures are essential to mitigate the risks of undue economic influence on political processes.

The interplay between economic power and social responsibility is increasingly relevant in contemporary discussions on corporate governance and sustainability. Companies are under growing pressure to balance profit-making with ethical considerations, environmental sustainability, and social impact. Corporate social responsibility (CSR) and environmental, social, and governance (ESG) criteria reflect a shift towards more responsible and sustainable business practices. The alignment of economic power with social and environmental goals is crucial for addressing global challenges such as climate change, poverty, and inequality.

Economic power isn't all sunshine and IPOs. The concentration of wealth can lead to significant inequality, creating a world where the top 1% own more than the rest of us combined. It's why some people are buying second yachts while others are struggling with rent hikes. Economic disparities can limit access to education, healthcare, and opportunities, perpetuating a cycle where those born into wealth stays wealthy, and everyone is left scrambling for crumbs.

Let's not forget the influence of economic power on politics. Lobbying, campaign donations, and good old-fashioned schmoozing mean that those with deep pockets often have the loudest voices. Policies that favour the rich aren't just accidents they're investments paying dividends. It's like the world's worst infomercial: "For just a few million dollars, you too can influence legislation!"

Economic power also manifests in the control over natural resources. Countries and corporations that control valuable resources such as oil, minerals, and arable land hold significant leverage in global markets and geopolitical relations. Resource-rich nations can use their economic power to influence global supply chains, trade policies, and international relations. However, the exploitation of natural resources also raises environmental and ethical concerns, highlighting the need for sustainable and equitable resource management.

Economic power is the ultimate wildcard in the game of life. It's the reason why some people fly private while others ride the bus. It's the driving force behind innovation, development, and occasionally, a whole lot of controversy. Whether it's corporations dictating market trends, banks managing your money, or tech giants mining your data, economic power shapes our world in ways we're only just beginning to understand.

The distribution of economic power within households and communities is another important dimension to consider. In many societies, economic power dynamics within families and communities are influenced by gender, age, and social norms. Women, in particular, often face systemic barriers to economic empowerment, including limited access to education, financial services, and employment opportunities. Empowering women and marginalized groups is essential for promoting inclusive economic growth and social equity.

Understanding economic power means recognizing the game and knowing that while the players change, the rules are always rigged in favour of those who have the most to lose. So, the next time you swipe your card, log onto a platform, or read about a million-dollar merger, remember:

In conclusion, economic power, defined by the control over wealth and resources, is a fundamental force shaping societies and influencing global dynamics. It encompasses various dimensions, including wealth accumulation, corporate influence, financial control, government policies, and technological advancements. The concentration and exercise of economic power have significant implications for social equity, political processes, and global development. Addressing the challenges and opportunities associated with economic power requires a comprehensive approach that promotes transparency, accountability, sustainability, and inclusive growth. By understanding and navigating the complexities of economic power, societies can work towards more equitable and prosperous futures.

Chapter 9

The Dark Side of Power: Corruption and Abuse

Power can be a bit like a superhero in a blockbuster movie—capable of great good but also prone to going full on villain mode when unchecked. On the one hand, responsible power can lead to amazing societal advancements, like ending poverty, curing diseases, or, more realistically, getting the pothole fixed outside your house. But let's not sugarcoat it power's dark side, filled with corruption and abuse, can turn things messy fast, like when the office potluck turns into a fight over who brought store bought guacamole.

Corruption is like that friend who always takes more than their fair share of the pizza but insists they didn't. It's the misuse of authority for personal gain, and it comes in many flavours: bribery, embezzlement, fraud, nepotism, and even that classic move where the boss hires their cousin for a job they're not qualified for. Corruption doesn't just siphon money; it sucks out public trust, makes governance as efficient as a dial up connection, and keeps inequality firmly in the driver's seat.

Think of corruption as a malfunctioning vending machine: you put in your money expecting a snack (or, you know, roads, schools, healthcare), but instead, it jams up, and you're left up banging on the glass. When power gets concentrated without checks and balances, it's like leaving that vending machine in charge itself—no oversight, just chaos, and sometimes a mysteriously missing Snickers bar. The more centralized the power, the easier it is for a few bad actors to treat public resources like their personal piggy banks.

Abuse of power isn't just about money; it's about wielding influence like a sledgehammer to get what you want, regardless of who gets hurt. It's the classic tale of bullies, whether in politics, business or everyday life, using coercion, intimidation, or good old-fashioned threats to get their way. Imagine the workplace tyrant who micromanages every decision or the politician who can't resist using their office to bend rules—it's not just frustrating; it's damaging to the course of institutions and communities.

Political corruption is perhaps the most egregious form. Think of politicians taking bribes like it's Black Friday at a luxury store or diverting funds like they're redirecting a GPS. It's the reason why some regions have bridges that lead to nowhere and public services that feel like they're stuck in the Stone Age. And don't even get started on rigged elections—it's like being promised a fair game of chess, only to find out your opponent brought a flamethrower.

Let's not forget our friends in the corporate world, where power abuse often gets the corporate gloss of "strategic decision making." Whether it's inside trading (trading secrets like they're collectible Pokémon cards), financial frauds, or cutting corners with worker safety, corporate corruption is like that shady guy at the poker table who keeps dealing himself aces. And when these powerful companies start throwing money on politics, it's like hiring a bouncer for the casino—they're not there to keep things fair.

Take the Enron scandal as a classic case of corporate corruption. Enron was the golden child of the energy world—until it was revealed that their "profits" were about as real as a Hollywood smile. Executives used accounting loopholes and fraudulent practices to inflate profits and hide debts. When the bubble burst, it wiped out shareholder value, led to thousands of job losses, and bought the phrase "cooking the books" back into fashion (not that anyone wants that kind of cookbook). Enron's top brass got rich while everyone else got the short end of the stick, proving that unchecked corporate power is like playing Jenga with dynamite.

The impact of corruption and power abuse is particularly pronounced in developing countries, where weak institutions and scarce resources make it feel like trying to build a house during a hurricane. Corruption siphons off funds meant for schools, healthcare, and infrastructure—like having termites in the foundation of progress. Imagine donating to build a new school, only to find out it went to the local official's sports car. It's the ultimate bait and switch, leaving the public disillusioned and stuck in a cycle of poverty.

Individuals who experience or witness such behaviours may become disillusioned with institutions, leading to decreased civic engagement and social cohesion. The psychological toll of living in corrupt or abusive environments includes stress, anxiety, and a sense of powerlessness.

Combating corruption and power abuse isn't easy, but it's not impossible—it's more like cleaning up after a frat party: daunting, but necessary. It starts with transparency, turning those smoke filled rooms into glass houses where every move is visible. Making government actions, financial transactions, and decision making processes public isn't just about nosiness, it's about accountability. Like grandma always said, sunlight is the best disinfectant.

Promoting transparency and accountability is key to combating corruption. Transparency involves making information about government actions, financial transactions, and decision-making processes accessible to the public. This enables citizens, civil society organizations, and the media to scrutinize and hold power holders accountable. Accountability mechanisms, such as audits and sanctions for misconduct, help deter corrupt practices and reinforce ethical behaviour.

Building a culture of integrity starts at the top. Leaders who model ethical behaviour, transparency, and accountability set the tone for others. It's like parents teaching kids that it's not okay to eat the entire cookie jar and then deny it while covered in crumbs. Ethics training, education, and emphasizing civic responsibility can help foster a society where honesty and integrity aren't just buzzwords—they're the norm.

Empowering citizens and civil society to engage in governance is another important strategy. Citizen participation in decision-making processes helps ensure power is exercised in the public interest. Civil society organizations can monitor government actions, advocate for reforms, and support victims of corruption and abuse.

The media plays a critical role in exposing corrupt practices and raising public awareness.

International cooperation is essential in addressing corruption and abuse of power, given their global nature. Transnational issues like money laundering, tax evasion, and illicit financial flows require coordinated efforts across borders. International agreements, such as the United Nations Convention against Corruption (UNCAC), provide frameworks for cooperation and the exchange of information. Global initiatives and organizations work to promote anti-corruption efforts and support reforms.

Technological advancements offer new ways to combat corruption, making the dark side of power easier to navigate. Block chain can make transactions as transparent as a glass bottomed boat, e-governance platforms can streamline government processes, and data analytics can spot shady patterns faster than you can say "Swiss bank account." But with great power (yes, even tech power) comes the need for safeguards to protect against misuse and ensure privacy and security.

The dark side of power, from corruption to abuse, poses challenges that threaten the very fabric of society. But by promoting transparency, accountability, citizen engagement, we can push back against the tide of corruption and foster more just and equitable communities. Remember, power isn't inherently bad—it just needs a good referee, an honest scoreboard, and maybe a little less money under the table. Together, we can keep power from going rogue and ensure it works for, not against, the public good.

In conclusion, the dark side of power, characterized by corruption and abuse, poses significant challenges globally. These negative manifestations of power undermine trust, justice, and development, affecting economic, political, and social well-being. Combating corruption and abuse requires comprehensive strategies promoting transparency, accountability, integrity, and citizen engagement. Through collective efforts and sustained commitment, it is possible to mitigate the dark side of power and foster more equitable and just societies.

Chapter 10

Empowerment and Personal Growth

Empowerment and personal growth are like life's ultimate power-ups! Imagine you're in a video game, and every time you level up, you learn new skills, make better decisions, and gain more control over your journey. It's not just about completing missions for yourself, but helping everyone around you crush their quests too. At the core of empowerment is the belief that you're the main character in your story, not just some sidekick waiting for life to happen.

When we talk about empowerment, we're not saying you'll suddenly have the power to fly or read minds (although, wouldn't that be cool?). Empowerment is about gaining control over your life, making informed decisions, and taking action to reach your goals. It's like upgrading from a bicycle to a turbocharged sports car you're still getting from A to B, but now, you're in control, and you're doing it with style!

Take Sarah, for example. She used to feel like her life was a series of "to-do" lists handed to her by others work, errands, more work. But one day, Sarah decided to take up painting, just because she liked it (and because paint-by-number sets counting as adulting, right?). Fast forward a year, she's selling her own artwork at local fairs. Sarah didn't just find a hobby she found her voice. That's empowerment.

Empowerment is also about collective actions. It's not just Sarah killing it at the art fair; it's about lifting up your friends and community, too. When empowered individuals come together, they can create social change. Think of it as a team-up in your favourite superhero movie only instead of battling aliens, you're tackling inequality and fighting for justice. Way cooler, right?

Social empowerment involves building supportive networks, fostering social cohesion, and challenging discriminatory norms and practices. Political empowerment entails participation in democratic processes, advocating for rights and justice, and holding leaders accountable. Psychological empowerment involves developing a sense of self-awareness, self-confidence, and resilience, enabling individuals to overcome adversity and achieve personal growth.

Personal growth is the lifelong journey of levelling up. Imagine it's like that never-ending quest in your favourite game (minus the annoying side quests like "sort out the laundry"), but instead of unlocking new weapons, you're unlocking better versions of yourself. Personal growth isn't about being perfect; it's about constantly learning, adapting, and realizing that your mistakes are just plot twists, not game overs.

The key ingredients to personal growth? Self-awareness, self-acceptance, and self-development. First, you've got to know yourself your strengths, weaknesses, and the weird things you do when no one's watching. Maybe you're good at starting things but not good at finishing them (we're all guilty of that half-knitted sweater in the closet). Understanding that about yourself helps you grow.

Next, you've to accept yourself. That's right flaws, quirks, and all. Self-acceptance is like finally upgrading to a phone case that fits it feel good to know you're right where you belong, even with all your cracks showing. And Self-development? That's the fun part where you decide what new skills to learn, what habits to build, and what heights to reach.

Let's look at Steve Jobs. He was fired from his own company Apple, the very company he founded! Talk about a plot twist. But did Steve crawl into bed with a pint of ice cream and give up? Nope. He went on to start another company (NeXT), which led him back to Apple, where he then introduced the world to the iPhone. Steve didn't see failure as the end he saw it as the ultimate learning experience and came back stronger than ever. That's personal growth at finest.

Life is full of curveballs, and personal growth is becoming like becoming a master at dodging, catching, and even throwing them back. Resilience is your ability to bounce back when life knocks you down, like those inflatable clown toys that just won't stay down no matter how hard you punch them. Whether it's a career setback, a personal loss, or a pandemic that turns your life upside down (looking at you, 2020), resilience helps you find your footing and move forward.

Adaptability, on the other hand, is like being a shape-shifter. It's the ability to change and evolve when circumstances do. When work-from-home became the norm, adaptable people embraced the chaos, turning their kitchens into office spaces and learning to juggle Zoom meetings with toddlers demanding snacks.

Developing a growth mindset is crucial. It's what allows you to see failure as nothing more than a chance to learn something new. People with a growth mindset are like the MacGyvers of life they can take a setback, mix in a little reflection, and turn it into something useful. They don't throw in the towel just because something didn't go as planned. Instead, they dust themselves off, take some notes, and get back to words.

Empowerment and personal growth don't just benefit individuals—they're good for society too. Think about it: empowered people who are committed to personal growth are more likely to get involved in their communities, stand up for justice, and even run for office. That's how societal change happens one empowered individual at a time, creating a ripple effect that leads to broader progress. And the best part? When you grow, you inspire others to grow too, like a contagious, feel-good superpower.

To truly foster empowerment and personal growth, we need to address systemic barriers everything from access to education and healthcare to challenging discriminatory norms. It's like trying to grow a garden you need good soil, water, and sunlight to thrive. Likewise, societies need supportive environments where people can grow without the weight of injustice holding them down.

Mentorship is another vital piece of the puzzle. A good mentor can be the Yoda to your Luke Skywalker guiding you, offering wisdom, and helping you navigate challenges. They don't have to carry a slight saber (though, that would be awesome) they just need to be someone who believes in you and helps you believe in yourself.

In the end, empowerment and the personal growth are the dynamic duo we all need in our lives. Empowerment puts you in the driver's seat, and personal growth is what keeps the journey exciting, challenging, and fulfilling. Whether you're painting masterpieces like Sarah or bouncing back like Steve Jobs, the road to empowerment and personal growth is paved with opportunities to learn, evolve, and make a difference in

Chapter 11

The Future of Power

The landscape of power is constantly evolving, shaped by technological advancements, social changes, and geopolitical shifts. As we look towards the future, several key trends and dynamics are likely to influence the distribution and exercise of power in the coming decades. Understanding these trends is essential for anticipating challenges and opportunities and shaping a more equitable and sustainable future.

Alright, strap in because the future of power is like the world's wildest rollercoaster only instead of loops and drops, we're dealing with tech revolutions, climate chaos, and geopolitical power struggles. It's a bit like playing chess, but on a moving train… that's also on fire.

First up, technology is basically sitting in the driver's seat of this crazy ride. From AI to biotech, the way power is used is shifting faster than your phone's software updates (which you still haven't installed). Think about it: today we've got robots that can deliver pizza at our doorsteps, algorithms that can predict your shopping habits, and smart homes that know you're out of milk before you do. But as cool as all that sounds, it's not all sunshine and rainbows. There's the small matter of privacy (hello, data breaches!), security (who's watching your baby monitor?), and ethical dilemmas (like, can a robot actually feel bad when it crashes your car?).

Sure, the digital age has given us the power to start global movements from our couches (#MeToo, anyone?). But it's also a double-edged sword. Misinformation spreads like wildfire, cyber-attacks are lurking around every digital corner, and don't even get me started at catfishing (sorry, not sorry, but no, that 6'4" model probably isn't texting you from a small town in Arkansas).

The future of power also has a serious people problem, and by that, I mean the world is filling up fast. Urbanization is making cities the new kings of the power jungle, with more people flocking to urban areas than ever. Picture this: by 2050, two-thirds of the global population could be city dwellers, and with many folks packed together, city councils are about to become the cool kids on the block. Think less "mayor of your small town" and more "superhero with a transit plan."

On the other hand, we're also getting older. I'm talking a lot older. Countries with aging population (like Japan) are facing massive healthcare and pension challenges. Imagine being in a country where walkers and Bingo halls are the hottest industries around. But here's the kicker: while older generations cling to traditional power structures, Gen Z is coming in hot with their TikTok-driven activism and "cancel everything" energy. It's going to be an interesting mix, to say the least.

Spoiler alert: climate change is about to flip the power dynamics on its head. The race to manage environmental disasters (because, let's be real, they're coming) will decide who holds the reins of power in the future. Nations that can adapt quickly and transition to a low-carbon economy will come out on top, while the rest of use might be stuck debating on who gets the last air conditioner.

Take the transition to green energy, for example. On one hand, it's a chance to create new jobs and build sustainable industries. On the other hand, there's the risk of countries clinging to fossil fuels like that friend who refuses to let go of their flip phone. And as rising sea levels swallow up coastlines, there's a new kind of real estate war brewing one where entire countries might be looking for a place to crash.

On the global stage, new powers like China and India are giving the traditional Western heavyweights a run for their money. It's like when the new kid at school sudden gets super popular and the old clique doesn't know how to handle it. Throw in regional powers like Russia and Brazil, and it's starting to look at a little chaotic. And unlike high school, this rivalry involves way more nuclear weapons and international treaties.

As new economic powers rise, the global power structure is looking less like a pyramid and more like one of those crazy Rube Goldberg machines where everything's connected and one wrong move could send the whole thing crashing down.

We can't talk about the future of power without mentioning the rise of social movements. Millennials and Gen Z aren't just updating their Instagram stories they're redefining what power looks like. Whether it's fighting for climate action, pushing for racial justice, or calling out corporations for shady practices, these movements are challenging traditional power structures. Remember the #MeToo movement? It wasn't just a hashtag it was global wake-up call. And that's the just beginning. The future of power lies in grassroots activism, where even a tweet can spark a revolution.

And let's not forget the power of persuasion. While military strength and economic clout are still big players., soft power winning people over with your charm and values is quickly becoming the name of the game. It's like being that smooth-talking friend who always convinces the group where to eat. Whether it's through cultural influence, diplomacy, or a really well-crafted Netflix series, soft power is how countries can win allies without firing a shot. Just ask South Korea, whose K-pop is conquering hearts globally faster than their missiles ever could.

The future of power will look less like a traditional battlefield and more like a spider web, with power flowing in all sorts of weird and unexpected directions. Governments, corporations, civil society everyone's going to be tangled in it. And no one's exactly sure who's in charge.

The future of power will be influenced by efforts to promote peace, security, and stability in a rapidly changing world. Conflict prevention, peacebuilding, and disarmament are essential for reducing the risk of armed conflict and promoting sustainable development. Diplomatic efforts to resolve conflicts, mediate disputes, and build trust among nations are critical for maintaining international peace and security. Investing in conflict prevention, peacekeeping, and peacebuilding capacities will be essential for addressing the root causes of conflict and promoting lasting peace.

The future of power will be shaped by efforts to promote sustainable development and environmental stewardship. Sustainable development goals, such as poverty eradication, climate action, and biodiversity conservation, provide a roadmap for addressing pressing global challenges and promoting prosperity for all. Transitioning to a green economy, investing in renewable energy, and adopting sustainable consumption and production practices are essential for achieving environmental sustainability and building resilience to climate change.

So, what's the takeaway? Buckle up. The future of power is going to be messy, unpredictable, and constantly shifting. But if you can keep up, there's a whole lot of opportunity to shape the world in ways we've never seen before. Just remember to keep your smartphone charged you're going to need it.

In conclusion, the future of power will be shaped by a complex interplay of technological, demographic, environmental, geopolitical, and social dynamics. Anticipating and responding to these trends will require foresight, adaptability, and collective action at local, national, and global levels. By promoting inclusive development, addressing systemic inequalities, and fostering cooperation and dialogue, societies can work towards a future that is more equitable, sustainable, and peaceful for all.

Chapter 12

Conclusion: Unravelling the Mysteries

In this journey through the enigma of power, we've delved into its origins, dynamics, and manifestations across history and society. From the ancient roots of power in human civilization to its modern-day complexities, we've explored the myriad ways in which power shapes our lives, relationships, and institutions. Along the way, we've encountered both the light and dark sides of power—its potential for positive change and progress, as well as its capacity for corruption and abuse.

Alright, buckle up because power is a wild ride and we're taking a deep dive into its inner workings! Imagine power as this sneaky, shape-shifting magician, who sometimes hands out world-changing tools, and other times, leaves a mess like a toddler with permanent markers. Throughout history, power has been the source of incredible good and, let's be honest, a lot of bad decisions too. (Looking at you, medieval kings with questionable fashion choices and a tendency to start wars).

First off, let's talk about the many faces of power. It's not just politicians waving from balconies or billionaires buying their fifth yacht. Nope, power operates on all levels from that one colleague who somehow always gets the best seat at meetings, to world leaders shaping global policies. It's a mix of political, economical, social, and psychological dynamics basically, a tangled mess, like your earphones after five minutes in your pockets.

Take the office dynamic, for example. Ever notice how Lisa from HR controls everything from coffee orders to who gets promoted? That's not just Lisa being bossy; it's a perfect mini-experiment in power. She didn't write the office rules, but she knows how to navigate them like a pro, using a mix of charm, knowledge, and possibly those donuts she brings on Fridays.

Now, here's a mind-bender: while power can be handed to you (looking at you, royals), what really matters is how you wield it. Just because you're sitting in the big chair doesn't mean you get to be Darth Vader. Or, well, you could be… but things won't end well for your empire (spoiler alert). The point is, power's like a double-edged sword use it wisely, and you're the hero of the story. Use it poorly, and, well, you're the villain in every fairy-tale ever.

And let's be real: we all think we'd be the good guy with power, but are we really turning down that last slice of pizza when no one's looking? Exactly. It's all about choice what you do with your power defines how it impacts others.

Here's the kicker: power doesn't act alone. It has a whole squad, including knowledge, wisdom, and morality. Think of knowledge as the brainy one, who reads all the instruction manuals and knows how everything works (your friend who actually reads the terms and conditions). Wisdom is the chill elder who tells you not to invest in bitcoin just because it's trendy. And morality? That's your inner Jiminy Cricket, reminding you not to do anything that would make your mom give you that look.

When these three team up with power, great things can happen like social justice movements and scientific breakthroughs. But if power ditches its squad, well, that's when things get a little House of Cards .

Speaking of, we can't talk about power without addressing the dark side. Corruption, abuse, exploitation it's all part of the deal when power goes unchecked. Imagine giving someone unlimited Wi-Fi with no data limits before you know it, they're downloading 20 seasons of reality TV and crashing the entire network. Unchecked power works just like that, except instead of wrecking your internet connection, it wrecks entire nations.

Whether it's a dictator clinging to control, or that one person in a group project who does nothing but still wants an A, power abuse is everywhere. The solution? Accountability. Transparency. And maybe a really good HR department to keep things in check.

But let's not get too gloomy. The best part about power is that it can be challenged and changed. History's full of people who've stood up to unjust power and won. Ever heard of Rosa Parks? Gandhi? Or that one barista who refuses to write your name wrong no matter how complicated it is? These people show us that even when power seems unstoppable, collective action can turn things around.

And here's the real kicker: sometimes the most powerful moves come from ordinary people like you, me, and, well, Lisa from HR when she's not being a meeting tyrant.

So, what's the takeaway here? Power isn't just about rulers, governments, or even Lisa and her doughnuts. It's about you . Power invites each of us to take a good, hard look at ourselves how we use it, how we give it away, and how we hold others accountable. It's not just some force out there controlling us; it's part of our everyday choices, interactions, and relationships.

Maybe it's as simple as asking yourself: how can I use my power (yes, even if it's just the power to decide what's for dinner tonight) to make the world a little bit better? And how can we, as a collective, unravel the tangled mysteries of power to create a future where everyone's empowered?

Because, at the end of the day, power is both the problem and the solution. And figuring it out? That's the ultimate puzzle.

Bibliography

Arendt, H. (1970). *On violence*. Harcourt, Brace & World.

Aristotle. (n.d.). *Nicomachean ethics*.

Aronson, E. (1969). *The theory of cognitive dissonance: A current perspective*. In L. Berkowitz (Ed.), *Advances in experimental social psychology (Vol. 4, pp. 1-34)*. Academic Press.

Asch, S. E. (1951). *Effects of group pressure upon the modification and distortion of judgments*. In H. Guetzkow (Ed.), *Groups, leadership, and men (pp. 177-190)*. Carnegie Press.

Bandura, A. (1986). *Social foundations of thought and action: A social cognitive theory*. Prentice-Hall.

Berrett-Koehler Publishers. Allen, D. (2001). *Getting things done: The art of stress-free productivity*. Penguin Books.

Branden, N. (1969). *The psychology of self-esteem: A revolutionary approach to self-understanding that launched a new era in modern psychology*. Jossey-Bass.

Brown, B. (2010). *The gifts of imperfection: Let go of who you think you're supposed to be and embrace who you are*. Hazelden Publishing.

Burns, J. M. (1978). *Leadership*. Harper & Row.

Carnegie, D. (1936). *How to win friends and influence people*. Simon and Schuster.

Carnegie, D. (1953). *How to stop worrying and start living*. Simon & Schuster.

Cialdini, R. B. (2009). *Influence: Science and practice (5th ed.)*. Pearson Education.

Cialdini, R. B., & Goldstein, N. J. (2004). Social influence: Compliance and conformity. *Annual Review of Psychology, 55*, 591-621. https://doi.org/10.1146/annurev.psych.55.090902.142015

Cialdini, R. B., & Trost, M. R. (1998). *Social influence: Social norms, conformity, and compliance*. In D. T. Gilbert, S. T. Fiske, & G. Lindzey (Eds.), *The handbook of social psychology (Vol. 2, 4th ed., pp. 151-192)*. McGraw-Hill.

Collins, J. (2001). *Good to great: Why some companies make the leap—and others don't*. HarperBusiness.

Confucius. (n.d.). *The Analects of Confucius*.

Covey, S. R. (1989). *The 7 habits of highly effective people: Powerful lessons in personal change*. Free Press.

Covey, S. R. (2004). *The 8th habit: From effectiveness to greatness*. Free Press.

Diamond, J. (1997). *Guns, germs, and steel: The fates of human societies*. W.W. Norton & Company.

Drucker, P. F. (1966). *The effective executive: The definitive guide to getting the right things done*. Harper & Row.

Elias, N. (1939). *The civilizing process: Sociogenetic and psychogenetic investigations* (E. Jephcott, Trans.). Blackwell Publishing. (Original work published 1939)

Flannery, K. V. (1972). *The cultural evolution of civilizations.* Annual Review of Ecology and Systematics, 3, 399-426.

Foucault, M. (1977). *Discipline and punish: The birth of the prison* (A. Sheridan, Trans.). Pantheon Books.

Foucault, M. (1978). *The history of sexuality, Volume 1: An introduction* (R. Hurley, Trans.). Pantheon Books.

French, J. R. P., & Raven, B. (1959). *The bases of social power.* In D. Cartwright (Ed.), *Studies in social power* (pp. 150-167). University of Michigan Press.

Gandhi, M. (n.d.). *The story of my experiments with truth.*

Gardner, H. (1995). *Leading minds: An anatomy of leadership.* Basic Books.

Gass, R. H., & Seiter, J. S. (2018). *Persuasion: Social influence and compliance gaining (6th ed.).* Routledge.

Gellner, E. (1983). *Nations and nationalism.* Cornell University Press.

Gilbert, E. (2015). *Big magic: Creative living beyond fear.* Riverhead Books.

Gladwell, M. (2008). *Outliers: The story of success.* Little, Brown and Company.

Goleman, D. (1995). *Emotional intelligence: Why it can matter more than IQ.* Bantam Books.

Greene, R. (1998). *The 48 laws of power.* Viking Press.

Greene, R. (2006). *The art of seduction.* Penguin Books.

Greene, R. (2009). *The 33 strategies of war.* Penguin Books.

Greene, R. (2012). *Mastery.* Viking Press.

Heider, F. (1958). *The psychology of interpersonal relations.* Wiley.

Heifetz, R. A., & Linsky, M. (2002). *Leadership on the line: Staying alive through the dangers of leading.* Harvard Business School Press.

Hill, N. (1937). *Think and grow rich.* The Ralston Society.

Kahneman, D. (2011). *Thinking, fast and slow.* Farrar, Straus and Giroux.

Kant, I. (1784). *An answer to the question: What is Enlightenment?* (H. B. Nisbet, Trans.). Penguin Books.

Kotter, J. P. (1996). *Leading change.* Harvard Business Review Press.

Kouzes, J. M., & Posner, B. Z. (2017). *The leadership challenge: How to make extraordinary things happen in organizations (6th ed.).* Jossey-Bass.

Lefebvre, G. (1967). *The French Revolution* (R. R. Palmer, Trans.). Columbia University Press.

Locke, J. (1689). *Two treatises of government.* Awnsham Churchill.

Lukes, S. (2005). *Power: A radical view (2nd ed.).* Palgrave Macmillan.

Machiavelli, N. (2005). *The prince* (W. K. Marriott, Trans.). The Floating Press. (Original work published 1513)

Mandela, N. (n.d.). *Long walk to freedom: The autobiography of Nelson Mandela.*

Mann, M. (1986). *The sources of social power, Volume 1: A history of power from the beginning to AD 1760.* Cambridge University Press.

Maxwell, J. C. (1998). *The 21 irrefutable laws of leadership: Follow them and people will follow you.* Thomas Nelson.

McNeill, W. H. (1982). *The pursuit of power: Technology, armed force, and society since A.D. 1000.* University of Chicago Press.

Milgram, S. (1963). *Behavioral study of obedience. Journal of Abnormal and Social Psychology,* 67(4), 371-378. https://doi.org/10.1037/h0040525

Newton, I. (1687). *Philosophiæ Naturalis Principia Mathematica.* Retrieved from [publisher or URL if available].

Nye, J. S. (2004). *Soft power: The means to success in world politics.* PublicAffairs.

Peale, N. V. (1952). *The power of positive thinking.* Prentice Hall.

Peterson, J. B. (2018). *12 rules for life: An antidote to chaos.* Random House Canada.

Petty, R. E., & Cacioppo, J. T. (1986). *Communication and persuasion: Central and peripheral routes to attitude change.* Springer-Verlag.

Pfeffer, J. (2010). *Power: Why some people have it—and others don't.* HarperBusiness.

Pink, D. H. (2009). *Drive: The surprising truth about what motivates us.* Riverhead Books.

Plato. (n.d.). *The Republic.* Retrieved from [publisher or URL if available].

Robbins, T. (1991). *Awaken the giant within: How to take immediate control of your mental, emotional, physical, and financial destiny!.*

Rousseau, J. J. (1762). *The social contract.* Penguin Books.

Schachter, S. (1959). *The psychology of affiliation: Experimental studies of the sources of gregariousness.* Stanford University Press.

Schwartz, D. J. (1959). *The magic of thinking big.* Prentice Hall.

Service, E. R. (1975). *Origins of the state and civilization: The process of cultural evolution.* W.W. Norton & Company.

Simon & Schuster. Canfield, J., Hansen, M. V., & Newmark, A. (2005). *The success principles: How to get from where you are to where you want to be.*

Sinek, S. (2009). *Start with why: How great leaders inspire everyone to take action.* Portfolio.

Socrates. (n.d.). *Socratic dialogues*

Tilly, C. (1990). *Coercion, capital, and European states, AD 990-1990.* Blackwell.

Tocqueville, A. de. (1835). *Democracy in America* (H. Reeve, Trans.). Saunders and Otley.

Tracy, B. (2007). *Eat that frog!: 21 great ways to stop procrastinating and get more done in less time.*

Tversky, A., & Kahneman, D. (1974). *Judgment under uncertainty: Heuristics and biases. Science,* 185(4157), 1124-1131. https://doi.org/10.1126/science.185.4157.1124

Vujicic, N. (2012). *Life without limits: Inspiration for a ridiculously good life.* Doubleday Religion.

Weber, M. (1947). *The theory of social and economic organization* (A. M. Henderson & T. Parsons, Trans.). Oxford University Press. (Original work published 1922)

William Morrow. Dweck, C. S. (2006). *Mindset: The new psychology of success.* Random House.

"Power is not about control; it is about the ability to influence. It isn't rooted in fear; rather, it is based on wisdom."

www.ingramcontent.com/pod-product-compliance
Lightning Source LLC
LaVergne TN
LVHW041541070526
838199LV00046B/1772